Frederick D. Hauptmann

Bread and Cake Baking

Frederick D. Hauptmann

Bread and Cake Baking

ISBN/EAN: 9783337531218

Printed in Europe, USA, Canada, Australia, Japan

Cover: Foto ©Lupo / pixelio.de

More available books at **www.hansebooks.com**

BREAD AND CAKE BAKING:

A

COLLECTION OF RECIPES

FOR MAKING

BREAD, CAKES, PIES, ICE CREAM, &C.

AND DESIGNED AS

AN ASSISTANT TO ALL INTERESTED IN BAKING.

BY

FREDERICK D. HAUPTMANN.

PITTSBURGH:

PRINTED BY STEVENSON & FOSTER.

1877.

PREFACE.

MY object in preparing this work for the public is, the recording of such information as I have gained by a practical experience of over ten years at bread and cake baking, ice cream making, &c., as will be of value to *all* interested in baking. Although there are a great number of bakers who do not *need* the book, I have no doubt that many of them will find something new. It is also hoped that the book will fill a vacancy felt by parents, who wish to place before their daughters a useful book on the art of baking, &c. The recipes are such as I have used, with the exception of a few given me by friends. While no extraordinary merit is claimed for the book, it is hoped, at the *very least*, that every purchaser will feel, after having tried some of the recipes, that he has received a *full equivalent* for his money.

Respectfully,

THE AUTHOR.

This book will be mailed to any address upon receipt of the price, $1.00, and can only be procured of the author, or by sending to his address.

F. D. HAUPTMANN,
P. O. Box 94,
New Waterford, Ohio.

BREAD AND CAKE BAKING.

REMARKS.

As this book is designed as an assistant to all interested in baking, I think it not out of place to call the attention of employers, journeymen bakers, and all persons connected with baking as a business, to a few of the evils existing at the present time. Hoping that there will be some remedy devised for them, that will be satisfactory to all rightminded persons concerned. The first I will mention is, the great number of hours employees in some bakeries are kept at work. The truth of the adage, "Man's inhumanity to man makes countless thousands mourn," is certainly apparent. Every person desires a few hours each day that he can call *his own*. I don't think that there is a journeyman baker but would be satisfied by having twelve hours as a day's work, nor do I think that any rightminded employer ought reasonably to demand more from him.

Another evil is the night work, and in many instances, working on Sunday. I believe this to be pretty generally, if not altogether, unnecessary. I do not wish it inferred by any remarks that I might herein make, that I wish to cast a stigma upon employers or any one else. Unprincipled persons may be found among all classes of people (at least as far as my observation has extended), and journeymen bakers, as a class, are no exception, for it is frequently found, after an employer has discharged a baker, that the baker has, before leaving, spoiled the flour or yeast. As in an instance that came to my notice, where a baker had put ashes in the stock yeast and ferment, and gunpowder in the malt.

There are in most of the large cities in the United States, what are known as " Bakers' Homes." The evil to which I wish to call the attention of all concerned, is the "treating" at these places. When a baker gets a situation and leaves there, he is generally expected to "treat the house," and if an employer hires a baker there it is likewise expected from the employer. I do not say that all " Bakers' Homes " are of this class, but there are a number of them. What is wanted is *sober, intelligent* workmen. While an occasional glass of ale or beer may benefit the person who indulges in it, or at the least do no harm, to get " on a drunk " certainly does not. Treating one another is a poor show of friendship ; but to meet together occasionally, and each one to express his opinion on various subjects connected with baking, &c., is for *the benefit of all concerned.*

The Bakeshop.

One of the evils about a great many bakeries is a miserable bakeshop. There is a tendency to too much show, in a number of bakeries. While the store and ice cream saloon may be fitted up grand, it is too often the case that the bakeshop is not fit to work in. I have seen bakeshops that were never scrubbed out, there being nothing but a few boards laid for a floor, or sometimes no floor but the ground. A bakeshop should be above ground, and not in the cellar, as I believe the majority of them are, and have enough windows to light up the shop well, and so arranged that plenty of pure air may be admitted. The shop should be kept warm or cool, as desired, and have some sort of flue or contrivance for carrying off to the top of the building the odors which arise from boiling hops, frying crullers, &c., when the shop is situated in the cellar, thereby preventing the store from being filled with them, which is sometimes the case. It should have a good hard wood floor, and so arranged that it may be easily scrubbed out, which ought to be done once every week, or *at least* once every two weeks. There should be a cupboard for all small pans and cake moulds.

A bake trough should be a little narrower at the bottom than at the top, and be made of hard dry wood. A large trough should be made of plank about two inches thick.

Bread.

Good bread should have a nice, soft, light brown crust, be white and spongy inside, and have an agreeable flavor. Too much yeast, or letting the dough get *too old*, will cause bread to crumble when cut. Take bread out of the pans as soon as baked, and stand it up edgewise on the bench or table; don't put on a pine table, as the bread will get a pine flavor. Cover up immediately with a thick cloth. Never put bread in the proof oven to raise. After it is put in pans, put in shallow wooden boxes, and cover by putting one box on the other, or put into a close cupboard. If you are sure of the heat of the oven, close the oven door when the bread is put in, and allow it to remain closed until the bread is about baked. The time it should be left in the oven will vary according to the size of the loaves, and the quality and lightness of the dough. The bread nearest the furnace will bake first; take that out when done, and change some of the pans around to where those stood that have been taken out, and proceed in this manner until all is baked. After the oven is heated, it should be allowed to stand with the dampers and doors closed for some time, from one-half hour to one and a half hours.

A barrel of flour (196 lbs.) will yield about 262 lbs. of baked bread, although it will vary a little according to the quality of the flour. To tell good flour, put a little in a cup or tumbler, add enough cold water to make a rather stiff dough, stir with a stick; if the dough is sticky it is bad. Good flour should be white, with a very pale straw-colored tint. A good idea is to use several brands of flour. Before buying flour smell it, to see that it is not musty.

Stock Yeast.

Before beginning to make yeast have the yeast tub or crock thoroughly scalded and aired. To do this, fill the tub or crock about one-fourth or one-half full of *scalding hot* water, cover closely, and let it stand about half an hour. Then scrub out thoroughly with a brush, rinse out well with clean cold water, and stand upside down in a cool shady place. Never use a tub or crock that has had grease in it, as the least bit of grease will spoil the yeast. It is a good plan to have an extra scrubbing brush for scrubbing out the yeast tubs, not using it for anything else, an extra dipper for taking the yeast out of the tub, and also a sieve for straining it. A hair sieve is the best. Good clear rain water is the best for stock yeast, but if that is not to be had, use any other that is clear.

To each "Patent Bucket" of water (holding about 2½ gallons) allow 2 oz. hops, 1 lb. flour, 10 oz. malt, and 1 pint stock yeast Put the water in a kettle, and when boiling briskly throw in the hops. Keep boiling briskly for about fifteen or twenty minutes, strain enough of the boiling hop water on the flour to make a stiff paste, stirring well with a paddle until right smooth, then strain on this the balance of the hop water, and set it away to cool. Stir it occasionally to hasten the cooling, or in summer set the crock in a tub of cold water, or take out some and put it into a tin bucket, and set this in cold water; when the whole of it is cool enough so that the hand can be well borne in it, put in the malt, stir it well, and let it set until about milkwarm. If the weather is very warm, let it get nearly cold. Then put in the stock yeast, stir well, and set in a warm place in winter: in the summer, set on the floor, in a corner of the bakeshop. If made in the morning, let it set until the next morning, or until it has *raised and fell.* It will not raise more than two or three inches. Then strain through a sieve into a clean bucket, rinse the tub or crock with cold water, and pour the yeast back into it again, and set it in a cool place, or on ice if the weather is very warm. Make this yeast twice a week, or if there is a great amount of baking to be done, and the weather is very warm, it is a good plan to make every other day.

Always taste the stock yeast before "stocking" the fresh away, to see that it is not sour; if sour, throw it away, and procure fresh from some baker who makes good bread. If the stock yeast is not to be had, put in six cakes of "National Dry Yeast," which is made at Seneca, N. Y. There may be others equally as good, but as I have used this I therefore recommend it. Should the yeast at any time appear to be *weak*, when making yeast again use a few cakes of the "National Yeast" along with the stock yeast that is used for "stocking" the yeast away with; or in the evening before making yeast, scald a little flour in a small bowl or crock, making a rather soft paste. When it is milk warm put in one tablespoonful of stock yeast to one pint of this. When it has fallen about half an inch or an inch, it is ready for use, and should not be allowed to stand long after that. Use about a half pint of this for "stocking" away two and one-half gallons of yeast. There are thermometers made especially for yeast, to show the degrees of heat, but in making this it is not necessary to use one.

Ferment.

Take 1 peck potatoes, wash clean, put into a kettle, and put on them 4 gallons water, or sufficient to scald 8 lbs. flour. When the potatoes have boiled soft put 8 lbs. of sieved flour in the ferment tub, and pour on enough of the boiling water to make a smooth, soft paste; or empty both the potatoes and water on the flour, and stir well with a stick or paddle, until the flour is all thoroughly scalded, after which pour on cold water until the hand can be borne in it, then squeeze all lumps fine with the hand and pour on more cold water until the mixture is milkwarm, or in warm weather nearly cold. Then put in 5 quarts stock yeast, and stir well. Make this in the evening and it will be ready for use by the next morning. It should stand in a moderately warm place. In winter use 6 quarts of stock yeast. Great care should be taken with this, as with stock yeast, to thoroughly scald the tubs, and not use anything that is greasy. This should *raise and fall* before it is used. It is best when made every day, but it can be kept several days in a cool place.

To Set Sponge.

To every three buckets of ferment use one bucket of water. Use milkwarm water in temperate weather. If the weather is very warm, set with cold water, or put just enough hot water into the cold to remove the *chill.* In very cold weather use the water as warm as the hand can be borne in it, and pour the water on the flour first, stirring around a few times before putting in the ferment. Use sifted flour for setting sponge and making dough. Set a rather stiff batter. Set the "span board" so that the sponge will raise nearly to the top of the dough-trough, but not touch the lid. Allow the sponge to fall two or three inches before beginning to make dough. Some bakers make dough as soon as the dough commences to fall, and others allow it to raise and fall twice.

Making Dough.

Use about three-fourths as much water for dough as you used ferment and water for setting sponge, providing you take no sponge out for anything else. For instance, when you set a "four-bucket sponge" add to this three buckets more water. Less water can be added, or more, the same as with setting sponge. If too little water is used, the dough will raise slow, and the bread will generally be dark, and if too much is used the dough will raise too fast, and will tear apart and appear to be *rotten.* Adding more or less water generally depends on circumstances, according to the weather, the amount of bread wanted, and the help. Always thoroughly mix the flour in the dough, cutting the dough in good-sized pieces with the scraper, and piling at one end of the trough; then pull the dough up at the sides of the trough, cut in pieces again, and pile to the other end of the trough. When well *mixed*, punch the dough with the fist, turn up at the sides, and throw to the other end of the trough again. Before throwing over the dough for the last time, sprinkle fine salt over the bottom of the trough; this will prevent the dough from sticking to the trough. A rather soft dough, well worked, will make the largest loaf of bread.

For hearth bread, make a stiff dough. Never use water that is warmer than milkwarm for making dough. The time dough should stand will vary, but generally requires from one-half hour to one and one-half hours. After the water is added to the sponge, mix the sponge well by squeezing with the hands, before adding the flour. Add ½ lb. salt to every 3 gallons of water. After the dough has raised well, cut in large pieces, punch together well, and throw out into shallow wooden boxes; then throw a piece on the bench, weigh into loaves and mould up round, dust a box with flour, put the loaves in it, and when they have remained in the boxes covered for fifteen or twenty minutes, put into pans, and put into shallow wooden boxes to raise, or set in a close cupboard. Don't set too close to the floor. Some bakers steam the bread, but the objections to this plan are that the pans become rusty. For my part, I prefer the shallow wooden boxes, and setting one box on another.

Rye Bread.

Take some of the wheat sponge after it has been thinned by the addition of the salt and water; add sufficient rye flour that has been sieved, to make a rather stiff dough. Let it raise well. Then throw out on the bench, work together, weigh into loaves, and mould round. Then lay a piece of coarse toweling on a board and dust it with flour. Roll out a loaf lengthwise, having it thick in the middle, lay at one end of the cloth, then pull up the cloth against this, and lay down another loaf, and so on. Lay the loaves upside down, cover them with a cloth ; if they raise too fast, remove the cloth. When they have raised sufficiently, dust slightly with flour and turn on the peel right side up, and with a sharp pointed stick make three or four holes in each loaf. Bake before bread, and bake on the hearth, and when taking out of the oven wash the loaves with a brush dipped in water. Don't set the loaves too close together in the oven.

French Bread

is made of wheat bread dough, set on cloths in the same manner as rye bread, but instead of rolling the loaf so it will be thick in the middle, have it rolled one thickness. Set in the oven, and wash over in the same manner as rye bread.

Graham Bread.

To each half gallon sponge after it has been thinned, add one-fourth pint of N. O. molasses, and add Graham flour to make a rather soft dough. Work the dough well, and let it raise well. Then throw on the bench and work together, and weigh off in loaves ; put in square tin or sheet iron moulds, and set in shallow wooden boxes. Bake the same as wheat bread, being careful that the oven is not too cold. Should the dough appear to crack, and tear apart after it remains in the pans a short time, it is generally on account of too little water being added to the sponge.

Twist.

Take out one-half gallon sponge after it has been thinned with the addition of the water and salt. Add about ¼ lb. soft butter. Make the dough a little stiffer than for bread. Let it raise well, then weigh off into pieces weighing about 1 lb. each. Pinch each piece in three equal pieces, mould them round and set on the bench, previously dusting the bench with flour. Let them remain about fifteen minutes, then roll out lengthwise, thin at the ends, and twist. Put them on pans and let them raise well, and bake before the bread. Grease over with a brush dipped in melted butter, when taken out of the oven. When making a large quantity, add a little scalded white corn meal; it will make them much whiter.

Buns.

Take out one-half gallon sponge before it has been thinned. Put into a wooden bowl, add 2 eggs, ½ lb. white sugar, a pint of warm milk or water, and about ¼ lb. of soft butter or lard, also a pinch of salt; add flour to make a soft dough, and work it well, let it raise well, then throw out on the bench, and punch together. Cut off with the scraper, and make into round balls. Put them on pans, and set them a good distance apart, put in the proof oven or a warm place to raise well; bake before the bread.

Rusks or Light Cakes.

Take of the same dough as mentioned for buns. Make the dough a little stiffer, allow it to raise well. Roll in the same manner as buns, making them smaller; set close together on a pan that has a high rim. Bake just after the bread is taken out of the oven.

Rolls.

Take out sponge before it has been thinned, add a little warm milk or water, a little soft butter or lard, a very little white sugar, and a pinch of salt. Make a rather stiff dough and work it well. Cover with a cloth, and allow it to raise well, then throw on the bench, punch together, and cut off with the scraper, and mould in small round balls. Set on the bench so they will not touch each other while raising, previously dusting the bench with flour. Cover with a cloth and allow them to set about fifteen minutes, then with a stick or the edge of the hand press down in the middle of each roll, and grease them by dipping a brush in melted butter, and greasing them in the middle; then turn over one side and press slightly with the hand.

Cinnamon Cake.

Take 5½ lbs. of the same dough as mentioned for buns, work in a handful of flour, and work the dough into nearly a square shape, a little longer than wide. Set on the bench, which should be previously dusted with flour. Allow it to remain about fifteen minutes, then roll out the size of the pan, which should be a large one, dust it slightly with flour, fold together, and lay on the pan, unfolding it again, then wash over with a brush dipped in warm milk and egg beaten up, or water and eggs. Sprinkle thick with granulated or coarse white sugar, and put little pieces of butter on the top, let it raise well and bake after the bread is taken out.

Wash to impart a gloss, to Buns, Rolls, &c.

Take a little white sugar and molasses, thin it by adding water. Dip a brush in this, and wash over the buns, rolls, &c., as soon as taken from the oven. If too sticky, more water should be added and not so much molasses.

Doughnuts.

Take bun dough, add a little flour; the dough should be a little stiffer than for buns, but not much. After the flour is worked in well, allow the dough to raise well, then throw on the bench, and work the dough into nearly a square shape. Roll about half an inch thick, cut out with a round cutter, and set in shallow wooden boxes that have been dusted with flour, and cover with another box, or lay on coarse cloths that have been slightly dusted. Cover with cloths, and when well raised fry in lard, turning them with a stick, and taking out with a skimmer, or a "lifter" made of wire.

Apple Cake

Is made of bun dough, rolled out in the same manner as cinnamon cake. Set slices of apples right close together on the cake. When the cake has risen sufficiently, beat up a few eggs, pour on some sour cream, sweeten with sugar, and flavor with cinnamon, or put on some cream cake custard. Be careful that the cake does not raise too much before putting on the apples and custard. Bake in a moderate oven.

Ferment, without Stock Yeast.

Make the ferment as heretofore mentioned, but instead of 8 lbs. flour use 4 lbs., and instead of using stock yeast put in 4 quarts ferment, or 5 quarts in winter. This ferment should be made every day. Throw in a small handful of hops in the kettle with the potatoes every other day, also a double handful of malt in the tub with the flour. Be careful not to have the mixture more than milkwarm before putting in the ferment, and allow the ferment to fall well before using. It will not generally raise very high. When sponge is set with this ferment it should be allowed to raise and fall twice before making dough. Always set as much of this ferment in a cool place as is wanted to start the fresh with.

Baking with Fleischmann's Compressed Yeast.

Dissolve 2 oz. compressed yeast in a little milkwarm water; be very careful not to have the water warmer than milkwarm. Put this in a bucket holding 2½ gallons water, and add enough milkwarm water to fill the bucket, being careful not to spill any. Set a soft sponge with this the evening before you wish to bake. In the morning add one-half or three-quarters of a bucket of milkwarm water to the sponge, and make dough; or make a ferment as herein mentioned, and instead of using stock yeast, use ¼ lb. of compressed yeast. Be careful in winter that the bakeshop does not get too cold. If using this yeast, always allow the sponge to *raise and fall twice* before making dough.

Where to procure Articles, Utensils, &c.

It is expected that this work will fall into the hands of many persons who wish to know where to procure articles and utensils for baking, making candies, cooking, &c. To all such I suggest to procure a copy of the "Confectioners' Journal," which is at present published at 501 Chestnut street, Philadelphia, and which will cost them probably 25 cents. Each number contains a collection of recipes and useful information for confectioners, bakers, cooks, &c.

Hints on Making Cakes.

Always have good flour and sieve it before using. Good packed butter is preferable to fresh for pound cakes, lady cakes, &c., as it can be beat lighter. When opening eggs, always open one or two at a time into a cup, and then empty into a larger vessel. By this method there will be no danger of having to throw away several dozen on account of a rotton one, or worse still, what is known as a "hay egg." The white of a hay egg resembles water, but is more greenish-looking, and has an offensive smell. One hay egg is sufficient to spoil 40 lbs. of pound cake batter. I remember of getting a part of one in a batch of "rough and readys." The cakes were put into the show case with other small cakes, and they tainted all the rest. Oil of bitter almonds, which is one of the strongest flavors for cakes known, will not remove the taste or smell of a hay egg.

Remember that cakes with molasses in, or a great deal of sugar, will be liable to burn easily. Before mixing cakes, always get everything ready for them (that is, if you have no one to assist you). First weigh the sugar, which should be sieved; then the flour, which should also be sieved. Mash soda with the pallet knife, and dissolve in the milk or water. Carbonate of ammonia should be pounded in a mortar, and sieved through a fine sieve, and kept in a wide-mouthed bottle or jar, tightly corked to exclude the air. Currants should be well washed in water, and then spread out thin on boards, and dried; when dried, put a few in the flour sieve, sprinkle a little flour on them, and rub around with the hand; pick out what stems will not go through the sieve. As a general thing, in making cakes the sugar and butter are well stirred together. The butter should be soft, but not melted. The eggs are worked in by degrees, two or three at a time, unless for a large mixture, then put in more. If the butter is hard, place in a warm room some time previous to making the cakes. If it is salty, wash it thoroughly, and press out all the water. For making cakes, have a wooden bowl of good hard wood, and nice and smooth inside. It is generally better to put cakes into the oven as soon as made, although some kinds can remain out a long time, as sugar cakes, &c. Allow cakes to cool before packing away.

Mix cakes in a bowl, stirring with the hand, unless for a small batch, then use a spatula. If you have a bakery, get walnut or tin trays made for cakes, lay the cakes in nicely, or stand on end if not liable to break; lay a sheet of paper on the bottom of the tray. There should be a sort of rack under the counter, where the trays will fit in nicely, and where it will be convenient to get at them when wanted. Cover the cakes with a cloth. Fill up a plate with each kind of cakes for the show case, by piling them up in a pyramid shape. The show case should always be well cleaned and polished, and before putting in the cakes, lay white paper on the bottom. Cakes that are sold by the slice should be cut through in the middle, such as citron, lady, Paris, &c. These cakes also present a very attractive appearance at the supper table, if cut in slices with a sharp knife, and nicely arranged on plates.

Pound Cake.

One lb. coarse pulverized sugar, ¾ lb. butter, 1 doz. eggs, 1 lb. flour, add a few drops oil of lemon. Stir the sugar and butter together until white and light, which will require twenty minutes or half an hour. Then put in 2 eggs, and beat them in pretty well. Scrape the mixture down from the side of the bowl with a pallet knife, put in two more eggs, and beat as before; and so continue on until all the eggs are in. Put in the oil of lemon, stir well, and scrape down as before. Then put in the flour. As soon as you see that the flour is well mixed in, put in moulds, and spread out smooth with the pallet knife, making the cake a little hollow in the middle, so that it will be more even when baked. The mould for a large pound cake should have a large spout; the cake will bake better, and is not so liable to be doughy in the centre. I have found good packed butter to be superior to fresh for pound cakes. Always line the moulds with a couple of thicknesses of brown paper for large pound cakes, and let them remain in the moulds over night, or until perfectly cooled. If the heat of the oven is "just right" for bread, and gives it a nice brown color, let the oven door open a short time about fifteen or twenty minutes after the bread is baked; then put in the pound cake—this is, if the oven is heated every day. If not, it will be necessary to put it in immediately after the bread. If the hearth of the oven is not level, slip a piece of wood under the mould, so the mould will stand level. If the butter is salty, wash it well in cold water, and work the water out well. The butter should be rather soft, but not melted. If the butter is hard, place in a warm room a few hours previous to making the cakes, or cut in small pieces, put in a pan, set the pan on the back part of the stove, and work with the hand until it is soft enough to be stirred with the sugar. When not baking bread, remember that a rather cool oven is required.

Lady Cake.

One lb. pulverized sugar, 1 lb. butter, 16 whites of eggs, 1¼ lbs. flour, 2 or 3 *drops* oil of bitter almonds. Stir the sugar and butter together until white and light, then add the whites of eggs by degrees, about three at a time, stirring well each time after they are put in. Put in the oil of bitter almonds, stirring it in well, mix in the flour lightly, and bake in a cool oven about the same as for pound cake. Care should be taken not to use more of the oil of bitter almonds than mentioned, as it is very strong and poisonous; but when used in so small a quantity it will do no harm, and if objectionable use oil of lemon instead.

Fruit Cake.

One lb. brown sugar, 1 lb. butter, 1 doz. eggs, 1¼ lbs. flour, 1½ lbs. seedless raisins, 1½ lbs. currants, 1 lb. citron cut in small pieces, 1 gill brandy, and one tablespoonful each of ground cinnamon, mace, allspice and cloves. Stir the sugar and butter together for a few minutes, then put in 2 eggs, stir a little, then 2 again, and so on until all the eggs are in: put in the spices and brandy, stir a little to mix well. Then put in the raisins, currants and citron, which should be first thoroughly mixed in a separate bowl. Put in the flour, and when it is well mixed in, put into moulds that have been well greased. The lard for greasing the moulds should be warmed just a little, so it can be laid on thick. Smooth the cakes out with the pallet knife, and bake in a cool oven. Bake after the pound cakes are taken out of the oven. Let the cakes remain in the mould until perfectly cold, as they are easily broken while warm. This cake will keep a long time, and is best when two or three months old.

Mountain Cake.

One lb. pulverized sugar, ¾ lb. butter, 8 eggs, 1 gill milk, a scant ½ teaspoon of soda, 1 teaspoon cream tartar, 1 lb. 3 oz. flour, a little extract of vanilla to flavor with. Dissolve the soda in the milk, put the cream tartar on a piece of paper. Stir the sugar and butter until white and light, add the eggs, 2 at a time, stirring well after they are put in (this cake does not require *quite* as much stirring as pound cake); then stir the milk and soda and add that and the vanilla, after which the cream tartar, and then immediately mix in the flour. Mix light; put this on three sheets of brown paper, an equal amount on each sheet. Spread in a round shape, about ½ inch thick, lay each layer of cake on a pan, and bake in a moderate oven. Be careful not to get the cake the least burnt, nor dried out too much. When cool carefully tear off the paper, and put between each layer of cake a thick layer of grated cocoanut and icing. The cocoanut and icing should be previously well mixed together. Use no acetic acid nor ultramarine blue for this icing, but simply the whites of eggs and sugar, well beaten together. Flavor with a little extract of vanilla. Trim the cake nice and round with a sharp knife. Have a clean, thin, round or square board, a little wider than the cake. Cut a piece of stiff white paper the size of the board, place this on the board and set the cake on. Brush away any crumbs that may be lying around the cake. Beat 15 whites of eggs right stiff, and add 1½ lbs. pulverized sugar, adding of it about ¼ lb. while beating. Mix the sugar in lightly with a broad, thin, wooden spatula, spread this evenly on the top and sides of the cake with the pallet knife. Put this in the oven a few moments to dry a little, but don't let it get brown. Ornament it by taking some of the icing that is left, putting in a gum sack, or one made of paper. Use a large star tube, like that used for almond puffs, to make the border. The other ornamenting should be done with a finer tube. When ornamented, dust a little with pulverized sugar, set on the peel and put in the oven. Let it remain there on the peel until a very delicate brown. The oven should be just hot enough to give it a very delicate brown color. The oven will be hot enough for some time after a batch of bread is baked. Be sure that the cocoanut is fresh and sweet, and don't remove the cake from the board, as the icing is easily broken, but set on the cake-stand with the board. Have the cocoanut and icing which is put between the layers a rather stiff paste. If it is too soft, the layers of cake are liable to slide. If too stiff, it does not taste as nice and dries out soon. This cake should not be kept longer than two or three days before it is eaten. The reason it is named Mountain Cake is, I suppose, because it is nice for pic-nics "on the mountain." However, by using enough layers, a mountain can be made of it.

Paris Cake.

$1\frac{1}{4}$ lbs. white sugar, $\frac{1}{4}$ lb. butter, 15 eggs, and the yolks of 8 more, $1\frac{1}{4}$ lbs. corn starch; beat the sugar and eggs together until when the beater is raised above the mixture, the mixture falling from the beater will lay on top of the other a few moments without sinking down. Have the butter melted to a thick oil. Take the beater out of the mixture, and put in a little oil of lemon to flavor, pour in the butter and stir with a spatula, after which mix in the corn starch, pour quickly in small pans. Have the mixture about $1\frac{1}{2}$ inches or 2 inches thick in the pans. The pans should hold from $\frac{1}{2}$ lb. to about $1\frac{1}{2}$ lbs. of the mixture. Put in the oven as soon as possible, which should be about the same heat as for sponge cakes, or a trifle hotter. After they are baked turn out of the mould on a tray, and when cool, ice over and mark in slices. This makes a splendid-looking cake when cut in slices with a sharp knife. Don't attempt to make a large cake of this mixture, as the butter will sink to the bottom of the cake, and it will not be fit to eat. Some bakers use ½ flour instead of corn starch.

Jelly Cake.

One lb. white sugar, ¾ lb. butter, 1¼ lbs. flour, ¼ oz. carbonate of ammonia, oil of lemon to flavor. Mix as mountain cake. Make four layers, and when baked put jelly between the layers, and trim nice and round with a sharp knife.

Large Sponge Cake.

One lb. white sugar, 1 doz. eggs, 1 lb. flour, a little oil of lemon to flavor. Beat the sugar and eggs together, until when the beater is raised above the mixture, the mixture falling from the beater will lay on top of the other a moment without sinking. Add the oil of lemon, mix in the flour lightly but thoroughly. Bake in a very moderate oven. Don't allow it to stand in the mould after it is baked.

Drop Cakes.

One lb. white sugar, ¾ lb. butter, 1 pint sweet milk or water, ½ oz. carbonate of ammonia, light weight, 2 lbs. 2 oz. flour, a little oil of lemon to flavor. Stir the sugar and butter together for about ten minutes; then add the eggs 2 at a time, and stirring well each time after adding them. When the eggs are well mixed in, put in the water and the flavor. Mix the flour in well, beating it in a little. Drop out with a tablespoon on pans that have been slightly greased, and bake in a medium hot oven. Should the hearth of the oven be very hot, so as to burn the cakes at the bottom, put the pan that the mixture is dropped out on on another pan. Good leaf lard can also be used; if using lard, use milk instead of water, and put in also a pinch of salt with the lard. These cakes also look well baked in small scalloped moulds (Patty pans). A few currants may be put on each cake if desired.

Lady Fingers.

One lb. white sugar, 1 doz. eggs, 1 lb. 1 oz. flour, a few drops oil of lemon. Beat the sugar and eggs together, until when the beater is raised above the mixture and run around, the mixture will lie on top a short time without sinking. Have ready a sack made in a conical shape, with an opening large enough to admit a tin tube without letting the tube slip through. Put a stopper of wood or a piece of paper in the tube, to prevent the mixture from falling through. Secure the sack to the bench by laying a 4 lb. weight on the corner of it. Open it out, and it is ready to put in the mixture. Have also some sheets of brown paper, a good quality of ordinary wrapping paper. Smooth out nicely, and cut a little smaller than the size of the pans. Also some pulverized sugar and a fine sieve. When the sugar and eggs are beaten as mentioned, put in the oil of lemon. Mix in the flour lightly but well. Mix the flour with the hand or a spatula. Fill the sack about three-fourths full of the mixture, and run out the lady fingers on the paper, in a long narrow shape, about 2 inches long, and

1 inch apart. Sieve pulverized sugar on immediately, and take the paper by the ends nearest you, lift up and let the sugar run to the other side. Then take the ends farthest from you, and lift the paper up altogether, so the sugar falls off. Put on the pan, and blow off any sugar that may be on the paper or pan. Bake in a pretty hot oven, until of a nice light brown color. Always run out the lady fingers and bake as soon as possible after the flour is mixed in, or they will crack on top and not look nice. When cool, turn over on the bench and wash over with a brush dipped in water. Spread with jelly and stick together. Always pick out two as near the same size as possible. Don't pile them high on a plate or tray.

Lemon Cakes.

1½ lbs. white sugar, 1 lb. butter, 4 eggs, ½ pint water, 3¼ lbs. flour, ½ oz., light weight, carbonate of ammonia. Flavor pretty strong with oil of lemon. Stir the sugar and butter together a few minutes, then stir in the eggs, after which add the water and oil of lemon. Mix in the flour lightly, and roll out in long rolls about the thickness of a broomstick. Cut in pieces about the size of a walnut with the scraper, and roll lengthwise with the hand; roll them so they will be thick in the middle and narrowing to a point at the ends. Throw on them coarse dry sifted sugar, press slightly, and lay on pans that have been slightly greased. Don't set close together, as they spread a great deal. Keep the sugared side uppermost. Bake in a pretty hot oven, to a very light brown color, being careful that they will not get burnt black at the bottom.

Sponge Biscuit.

One lb. white sugar, 1 doz. eggs, 1¼ lbs. flour, ¼ oz., strong weight, carbonate of ammonia, oil of lemon to flavor. Beat the sugar and eggs together about the same as for sponge cake; when beaten as described, add the carbonate of ammonia and oil of lemon, stir in well with the beater, after which mix in the flour, and drop out with a spoon on very slightly greased pans. Drop small and a good distance apart from each other. Bake in a rather cool oven, and as they are taken out of the oven cut them loose from the pans with a pallet knife. These are nice cakes, but they dry out soon, and therefore should be baked very light.

Cream Puffs.

One lb. 2 oz. flour, 10 oz. best leaf lard, 1 qt. water; let the water and lard come to a boil in a sauce pan. As soon as the lard is melted, which may be known by stirring with a spatula (have the flour sieved and in a scoop ready to put in), and while the lard and water is boiling briskly, with the left hand set the pan on the edge of the stove, and with the right empty in the flour immediately, and stir right brisk for a few minutes with a spatula. Take off the stove and put in 3 eggs and a scant ½ oz. carbonate of ammonia; stir well. It will require about 20 eggs, putting in 3 at a time. Scrape the mixture down from the sides of the pan, and stir thoroughly each time 3 eggs are put in. When 18 of the eggs are in, drop a medium heaped tablespoonful of the mixture on a pie plate and put in the oven. Should the cake remain small and not raise much, stir in more eggs, being careful not to get in too many, as in that case the cakes will run out flat. Drop on pans very slightly greased, a good distance apart, and bake in a hot oven (just before putting in bread). If not baked sufficiently, they will fall shortly after being taken from the oven When baked take a thin sharp knife and cut in at the side of the cake, about half way through. Hold the cake up sideways in the left hand, holding the top up with the thumb and finger, and put in a tablespoonful of custard with the right. They will not keep more than about a day in the summer when filled with custard.

Custard for Cream Puffs.

One-half gallon sweet milk, ¾ lb. white sugar, 9 eggs, ½ lb. corn starch or flour. Stir the sugar, eggs and corn starch together until smooth. As soon as the milk boils pour this in quickly, and set to the edge of the stove. stirring briskly with a paddle, to prevent burning, When cool flavor with vanilla or lemon.

Small Sponge Cake.

One lb. white sugar, 1. doz. eggs, 1 lb. 1 oz. flour, a few drops oil of lemon. Beat the sugar and eggs together until when the beater is raised a little above the mixture, and run around, the mixture falling from the beater will lay on the top of the rest for a moment without sinking right away. Mix in the flour light but thoroughly. The moulds should be a little longer than wide, and hold about a tablespoonful. Bake in a medium hot oven.

Cup Cake.

1½ lbs. white sugar, 1 lb. butter, 1 pint eggs, 1 pint sweet milk, 2¾ lbs. flour, the weight of one copper penny of soda and two of cream tartar. Put into round tin moulds holding about ½ lb. each, and bake in a moderately cool oven.

Brown Scotch Cake, No. 1.

Two lbs. brown sugar, 1 lb. butter, 4 eggs, ½ teaspoon soda, a very little water—about ½ gill—2¼ lbs. flour. Flavor strong with ground cinnamon. Mix and cut out rather thin with a square cutter. Don't roll out much of the mixture at a time, as it is *short* and rather hard to cut out, and don't set the cakes very close together on the pans. Grease the pans very slightly, and bake in a moderate oven to a nice brown color.

Brown Scotch Cake, No. 2.

Two lbs. brown sugar, ½ lb butter, 3 lbs. flour, a little ground cinnamon, enough molasses to make a rather stiff dough. Roll and cut out with a round cutter. Grease the pans slightly, and bake in a moderate oven.

White Jumbles.

One lb. 2 oz. white sugar, 10 oz. butter, 1 pint water or sweet milk (scant measure), a very little carbonate of ammonia, about a scant ½ oz., 4 eggs, oil of lemon, 2¼ lbs. flour. Stir the sugar and butter together a few minutes, then put in the eggs, 2 at a time, stirring them in well. Add the carbonate of ammonia, and oil of lemon and water, stir a little and add the flour. Don't mix more than is necessary to get the flour mixed in, or they will be tough. Squeeze through a sack in the same manner as lady fingers, substituting a "jumble tube" instead of a plain one (a plain one will do). Form into large rings on pans that have been very slightly greased. If squeezed through a "jumble machine," about ¼ lb. more flour should be added, and then make in long strips on the bench, previously dusting the bench with flour. Cut in strips 4 or 5 inches long, and lay on the pans, forming rings. Bake in a hot oven, and slip another pan under each pan of jumbles before putting in the oven, to prevent them from burning.

Brown Jumbles.

Brown sugar 1½ lbs., lard ¾ lb., 6 eggs, ½ oz. carbonate of ammonia, 1 pint sweet milk, 3¼ lbs. flour, about ½ oz. ground cinnamon. Stir the butter and sugar together, add the eggs, 2 at a time, stirring well each time after they are put in; then add the carbonate of ammonia, milk and cinnamon. Stir well and mix in the flour. Don't mix longer than is necessary to have it well mixed in. Sift a little granulated sugar on the bench, and press the mixture through a jumble machine on the sugar in long strips. Cut in pieces about 4 or 5 inches long, forming rings, and set on slightly greased pans, keeping them a good distance apart, and keep the sugared side of the jumbles uppermost. Bake in a moderately hot oven.

White Scotch Cakes.

1½ lbs. white sugar, 1 lb. butter, 4 eggs, a little over a gill sweet milk or water, ¼ oz. carbonate of ammonia, 2½ lbs. flour, and a little oil of lemon to flavor. Stir the sugar and butter together, add the eggs, stir well, then the carbonate of ammonia, milk and oil of lemon, after which the flour. Mix and roll out thin, and cut out with a rather small round cutter. Don't roll out much of the mixture at a time, put on slightly greased pans, and bake in a cool oven.

Wine Cake.

Four lbs. pulverized sugar, 2 lbs. butter, 2 doz. eggs, 2 oz. soda, 4 oz. cream tartar, 2 qts. sweet milk, 1 qt. water, as much flour as will make a soft dough. Mix as pound cake, but not stirring as much. Beat the flour in well, and flavor with oil of lemon, or leave out a little of the water, and substitute wine. Put in round moulds, holding about ½ or ¾ of a pound of the mixture; moderately cool oven.

Molasses Cup Cake.

One qt. N. O. molasses, 1 doz. eggs, 1¾ qts. sweet milk, 1 oz. soda, and 1 oz. carbonate of ammonia; a little butter or lard may be added. Flavor with oil of lemon. Put in enough sieved flour to make a soft dough, being careful not to get it too stiff. Beat the flour in well, and bake in small scalloped moulds in a moderate oven.

Taylor Cake, No. 1.

One-half lb. brown sugar, ¾ lb. butter, 6 eggs, 1 qt. New Orleans molasses, a scant pint of water, 2 oz. soda, about ½ oz. ground ginger, and ¼ oz. ground allspice, 3½ lbs. flour. Stir the sugar and butter together for a few moments, then add the spices, molasses, water and soda. Stir well, and then put in the flour; when well mixed in, put in the eggs, and stir the mixture right well, scraping down from the sides of the bowl occasionally with the pallet knife. Drop on slightly greased pans, or in Patty pans, and bake in a moderate oven. Bake light, as they are easily burnt at the bottom.

Taylor Cake, No. 2.

Stir the sugar and butter, add the 60 eggs by degrees, adding 8 instead of 6, beating up well, then put in the molasses, spices, water and soda. Stir a little, and then put in the flour. Mix lightly. Bake as No. 1.

Chocolate Sponge Drop.

Make a mixture the same as for lady fingers, and squeeze through the "lady finger sack" on brown paper, making small round cakes; but don't sieve sugar on them. Bake in a medium hot oven. When baked and cool, wet the paper with a brush dipped in water, and take off the cakes. Cut the cakes to one size with a cake cutter, or trim with a sharp knife. Lay two of them together, putting jelly between. Put in a small kettle 2 lbs. white sugar, ¼ lb. cocoa, cut fine, and add ½ pint water; boil to a thread, which may be known by taking a little between the thumb and finger and pulling apart; when a thread about an inch long can be drawn in this manner, it has boiled sufficient. Take from the fire, and with the spatula keep rubbing the mixture well against the sides of the kettle, until pretty thick, which will be in about five or ten minutes. Have the cakes and a few greased pans ready at hand, also a piece of wire bent in the shape of a pair of tongs. Throw in the cakes one at a time and take out with the wire, holding the cake against the wire with the left forefinger. This should be done as soon as possible, as the chocolate will soon harden. Set on the greased pans, trim off any lumps of chocolate that may be hanging to the cakes, and set on a tray. Large cakes may be covered with chocolate by first putting a plain border of icing around the cake, using a large tube, that is, in case the cake should be high in the middle, but if flat as jelly cake, spread out the chocolate immediately with a pallet knife.

Jelly cakes covered with chocolate, and finely ornamented, produce a fine effect. The chocolate that is left over may be used again by adding more cocoa and sugar; but in using that which is left with fresh, it is best to put in about ¼ lb. *Fondant*, after the sugar and cocoa are boiled to a thread, and before rubbing against the sides of the kettle. The quantity of sugar and chocolate herein mentioned is sufficient for a 1 lb. batch of the cakes.

Jenny Lind Cakes.

Take lady cake mixture and squeeze through a "lady finger sack" into small round cakes about the size of a large hickory nut, on pans that have been slightly greased. Let them be a good distance apart. Lift the pan up about a foot or two and let it fall down flat on the table to flatten the cakes a little. Be careful to have pans that are smooth and even. Bake just before lady cake, as they require an oven a trifle hotter. When baked, the cakes should be nearly white, with a nice brown edge. When cool, make a star, ring, heart, or other design on each cake, with Meringue icing or ornamenting icing, and fill the space inside of the design with nice red or amber colored jelly; squeeze the jelly through foolscap paper, making it cone-shaped Fill with jelly, and then cut off the end. Be careful not to get the cakes baked too much.

Jelly Roll.

One-half lb. white sugar, 14 eggs, ½ lb. flour. Beat the sugar and eggs together until stiff, mix in the flour, and spread on a sheet of brown paper that has been laid on a pan. Spread about ¼ or ½ in. thick. Bake in a moderately hot oven. When baked, turn over on another piece of brown paper laid on the table, and wash over with a brush dipped in water, spread with jelly and roll up quick. It must be spread and rolled as quickly as possible after it is taken out of the oven. If the jelly is too thick, stir it so it will spread nicely.

Molasses Pound Cake.

One quart New Orleans molasses, 1 qt. milk or water, 1 oz. soda, strong weight, 6 eggs, 6 oz. butter, 6 oz. lard, 2 tablespoonfuls ginger and one of allspice, 4 lbs. flour.

Have the butter a soft paste, stir in the eggs well, mash the soda and dissolve in the milk, put in the flour. Don't mix it more than is necessary to mix it in. Put in medium size pans, and bake in a cool oven.

Rough and Readys.

One-half lb. brown sugar, ½ lb. butter or lard, ¾ pint molasses, ¼ pint milk or water, light ½ oz. soda, 1 tablespoon ground cinnamon, 1 teaspoon ground allspice, 4 eggs, flour enough to make a dough that can be nicely rolled out, about 2 or 2¼ lbs. Dust a clean board very lightly with flour, cut out the cakes about ¼ inch thick, and a long shape. Set closely together on the board, beat a few yolks of eggs with a little sweet milk or water, and with a brush dipped in this wash over 2 or 3 doz. of the cakes at a time. Throw them over on dry granulated sugar, and set on slightly greased pans; bake in a moderate oven. If desired, about ½ lb. flour less may be taken, using instead ½ lb. scrap cakes.

Ginger Snaps.

One lb. brown sugar, 1 lb. butter or lard, 1 quart N. O. molasses, 1 pint water, 2 oz. soda, 4 oz. ginger. Mix and cut them out with a small cutter, about the size of a large copper cent; or cut and roll in long round pieces a little thicker than a broom stick, cut in small pieces with the scraper, make them into round balls by rolling one in each hand in the same manner as light cakes. Set on pans far enough apart so they will not run together, and flatten each one with the palm of the hand. If they are desired extra *hot*, put in a little cayenne pepper. The pans should be greased lightly. Bake in a moderate oven.

Ginger S's.

One lb. brown sugar, 1 lb. lard, 1 quart N. O. molasses, 1 oz. soda, ½ pint water, 3 oz. ginger, about 5 lbs. flour. Mix and cut in small pieces as described for ginger snaps. Roll each small piece lengthwise until a little thicker than a lead pencil, then form into shape something like a letter S, put on slightly greased pans, and bake in a moderate oven.

Crullers.

1¾ lbs. white sugar, 10 eggs, ¼ lb. butter, 1¾ pints sweet milk, good measure, 1 teaspoonful soda, 2 teaspoonfuls cream tartar, 4¾ lbs. flour, a little oil of lemon to flavor with. Dissolve the soda in the milk. Have the butter soft. Mix the sugar, eggs, butter and oil of lemon together, stir in the soda and milk, then put in the flour, and sprinkle over it the cream of tartar. Mix and cut out in small narrow rings, about ¼ inch thick. Spread dry cloths on boards and lay the crullers on these, or lay them on boards that have been slightly dusted with flour. They should be fried in hot lard as soon as possible after being mixed and cut out. Have *plenty* of lard to fry them in. Turn them over with a stick. When done frying set the lard in a cool place, and before frying again set the vessel with the lard on the stove for a moment, and turn out the lard on a piece of paper laid on the bench or floor. Scrape off that which is black, clean out the vessel, and put in the lard again with more fresh lard.

Scrap Cake.

Three lbs. scrap (trimmings off jelly cakes, and various other kinds of cakes that will not sell, but are good yet, rolled and sieved), ½ gallon N. O. molasses, 1 quart sweet milk, 1 oz. soda, ½ lb. butter, about 1 oz. ground ginger and ½ oz. ground allspice, a few currants, and flour sufficient to make a medium stiff dough Mix and spread about 1½ inches thick in a pan that has been right well greased. Bake in a cool oven, and when cool ice over with water icing.

Citron Cake.

Make a mixture for pound cakes as mentioned, and just before putting in the flour add ½ lb. citron, cut in fine pieces, and 1 lb. currants. Mix and bake as pound cake, in a square pan. When baked turn out on a tray, and when cold, ice and mark in slices.

Currant Cake.

Make the same as citron cake, but instead of the citron take currants, and bake in round moulds. When cool, ice and mark in slices.

Ginger Cakes.

One-half gallon N. O. molasses, 1 pint water, 2½ oz. soda, 4 oz. ginger, 7¼ lbs. flour. Mix light, cut about ¼ inch thick. Put on pans that have been slightly greased, and before putting in the oven wash over with a thin wash made of molasses and water. Bake in a hot oven.

Sugar Cakes.

One lb. white sugar, ½ lb. butter, 2 eggs, ½ pint water, ¼ oz. carbonate of ammonia, oil of lemon to flavor. Mix, cut out in cakes about ¼ inch thick, and bake in a hot oven.

Macaroon Pyramid.

For this it is necessary to have a round tin mould or form of a conical shape, wide at the bottom and narrowing to a point at the top; have also a round flat ring cut out of a piece of tin, that can be put over the top of the mould and slipped half way or three-quarters down; the mould can thus be used for a large or small pyramid, as desired. If the mould is a new one, scrub off well with hot water and soap, wipe dry, and when cool grease with a brush dipped in lard. Don't have the lard too hot, just soft enough so it can be applied with a brush; grease the mould well. A macaroon pyramid looks best if the macaroons are uniform, about the size of a silver quarter, or a little larger. If some of them should be larger than others use them for the bottom of the pyramid. Pick out all the best that are wanted for the pyramid.. They should be firm on the bottom. If hollow at the bottom or cracked much on top, the pyramid will be liable to break when lifting off the form.

Take about 3 lbs. of white sugar, the brand known as "A," water enough to barely cover it, then put into a small copper or brass kettle, or a stew pan will answer; being careful to have the vessel used right clean. When it commences to boil, cover with a clean board or sheet of tin. Or after it commences to boil, wash down the sides of the kettle occasionally with a clean white rag dipped in a bowl of cold water, and wrung out a very little. Add while boiling 1 teaspoon cream tartar. When boiled to a crack it is done and should be taken from the fire, and set into a larger vessel that has very little water in it, to prevent the sugar from coloring or scorching from the heat of the kettle. Now take a macaroon in the left hand and hold it against the bottom of the form, and take another in the right hand, dip the edge in the sugar (being careful not to burn the fingers) and stick it against the other macaroon. Keep on in this way until there is a row of macaroons around the form. Dip the macaroons close to the side of the kettle, where the sugar is the thickest. Now set more macaroons above this row, building around the same as the first row, but dipping the macaroon so it will stick to the row beneath as well as to the side. When three rows are built around in this way, loosen them by lifting up just a very little to see that it is loosened. If it is intended for a large pyramid, take a small stick, put a little more sugar between the rows before loosening, so it will be firm. This is only needed to be done with the three lower rows. When about half built loosen again, and also when about three-fourths built. Proceed in this way until within about two inches of the top of the form, making the top row even all round by taking pieces of macaroon or very small macaroons. Pour enough of the sugar on a marble slab or pan that has been greased, to make a small round cake, fasten this with some of the sugar on top of the pyramid after the pyramid has been lifted from the form. When lifting off be careful not to strike the top against anything. If it will not loosen easily, light a small piece of newspaper and put under the form. Place a hand on each side of the pyramid and raise it up. If it does not come loose in this way, get an assistant to hold a 4 lb. weight on top of the form to hold it firm until loosened, and be careful not to push against it when lifting. Try to have it set up as soon as possible, as the sugar will soon harden. If it is commencing to harden set on the edge of the stove to keep warm, or add about ½ pint water, and boil to a crack as before. When the pyramid is set up it may be ornamented with ornamenting icing, and composition flowers, gilt, silvered and green leaves. Macaroon pyramids will not keep nice long in warm or damp weather, and are therefore mostly made in the fall or winter.

Candy Ornaments for Macaroon Pyramid.

Cut a design out of pasteboard according to your fancy. Grease a marble slab, and with a lead pencil mark off the design on the slab. Ornament over the lead pencil mark with ornamenting icing, using a plain coarse tube. Run inside of this sugar that has been boiled to a crack, using a small copper pot with a long fine spout, or make a fancy design on the slab with the lead pencil, and run out boiled sugar with a spoon. As soon as the designs harden loosen with a pallet knife, being careful not to break them, or fasten to the pyramid orange slices that have been dipped in boiling sugar, first dipping in one end, letting it harden, and then the other. Be careful not to tear the fine skin around any of the slices.

To Make an Egg Beater.

Take some stout brass wire, and cut into lengths of about 2 feet, or as long as desired. Take 8 or 10 of these, and bend them in the shape wanted. Wrap the part wanted for a handle tightly with stout cord. A stick of wood may be used for making the handle stronger, but if stout wire is used and wrapped well it will answer the purpose. If the beater is wanted for beating the whites of eggs alone, thinner wire may be used.

Almond Puffs.

The whites of 7 eggs, 1 lb. pulverized sugar, 2 oz. blanched almonds, dried, rolled, and passed through a sieve. Let off the whites into a clean round-bottomed copper kettle, or a tin bucket, beat with the beater until right stiff, occasionally adding a tablespoonful of the sugar while beating, then put in the sugar and almonds, and mix with a thin wooden spatula. Mix light, then pass through a gum sack made in the same manner as a lady finger sack, first slipping in a tin tube. Squeeze through this on pans that have been well cleaned and thickly greased. Put in a very cool oven. When they have a crust so they can be well handled take them off the pans and put on tin trays.

Icing.

Let off the whites of 8 eggs into a clean white bowl, or let them off into a cup one at a time and then empty into the bowl. Be careful not to get the least particle of yellow in the whites. Add a few drops of acetic acid to the whites of eggs, and as much ultramarine blue as will lay on the point of a penknife; great care should be taken not to get in too much or the icing will be blue. Stir in enough pulverized sugar that has been passed through a fine sieve to make a thickish paste. Beat this up by holding a spatula in each hand, having the bowl in the lap or standing on a bench or table, beat until right white and light, which will require brisk beating for 20 minutes. The icing should be just thick enough so that it can be spread with a pallet knife nice and smooth on a cake without running off the sides while the cake is drying. Spread the icing within about half an inch of the edge of the cake. Put in the proof oven, or dry inside the oven after the baking is done. Be careful that the icing don't get brown. As soon as the icing is dry enough to bear the weight of the ornamenting that may be put on, take the cake out. This amount of icing is sufficient to ice and ornament a good sized cake. If the icing is wanted for ornamenting also it should be made of "lozenge sugar," which is fine like flour; but for plain icing alone the common pulverized sugar will answer. Be careful to have the bowl, paddles, &c., right clean, and see that they are not greasy.

To ice and ornament a small cake, it is best to make plain icing, and then give the cake one thick coating of icing, and add sufficient sugar to make the icing stiff enough for ornamenting. But for a large cake, as a wedding cake, give the cake a very thin coating of icing, allow this to dry, then put on a thick coating of icing and allow that to dry also; beat up icing in a separate bowl for ornamenting the cake. This icing should be so that it will stand alone, and that the *border* will not slip off the cake after it is put on.

To become a good ornamenter requires a great deal of practice; and to become a first-class one a knowledge of drawing is necessary, although any one with a little practice can ornament a cake so that it will look well. Take a piece of ornamenting paper, or writing paper will do, wrap it around the hand or fingers so as to form it into a conical shape, then holding in the hand so that it does not unwrap, cut off the pointed end with a scissors, and slip in an ornamenting tube at the top. Put in the icing, turn the paper down, and squeeze with the ball of the thumb. Ornamenting tubes are cut in different designs. Use a coarse tube for making a border around the cake, and a fine one for ornamenting inside of the border. Gilt, silvered, and various colored leaves can also be put on; also a variety of ornaments. Before beginning to ice a cake always trim it neatly with a sharp knife, so that it will have a nice shape, or use a large grater. Clean off the crumbs well with a brush, and fill up the hole made by the spout of the mould by firmly fastening a hard sugar or other cake in it. Always use white icing and white ornaments for decorating a wedding cake.

Water Icing.

Take pulverized sugar and water, and make a rather thick paste, add a few drops oil of lemon, spread on the cake and set the cake in a warm place a few minutes to dry.

Substitute for Whites of Eggs in Making Icing.

Three ounces isinglass, ½ lb. white glue, 2 gallons water, boil this together and skim well. Put in afterwards ¼ lb. burnt alum, which has previously been dissolved in warm water. Keep in a cool place. Cakes iced with this should not be allowed to stand over a day or two, as the icing soon becomes very hard.

Soda Biscuit, No. 1.

Eight lbs. best flour, 1 lb. lard, ½ oz. soda scant, ½ oz. carbonate of ammonia, ¼ lb. cream tartar, ½ gall. milk, about 1 pint water; mix. Cut out thick and bake in a hot oven, leaving the oven door partly open; add also a little salt to the flour, &c.

Puff Paste.

To make good puff paste, it is necessary to have the best of flour and good fresh butter. The butter should be pretty stiff, but not hard. If the butter is soft, put it in ice water two or three hours previous to making the paste. Take 2 lbs. flour, and 2 lbs. butter; mix a small piece of the butter, about ¼ lb., with the flour, by rubbing it thoroughly between the palms of the hands until fine. Put in 1 pint ice water, or some that is right cold. Mix and work this well in a bowl, then roll out on the bench until about half an inch thick. Work the balance of the butter with the hands in a little cold water. Then work out the water by taking a little of the butter in the left hand, and slapping it with the palm of the right hand. Lay this butter evenly over the paste to within about 1 inch or 1½ inch of the edge of the paste. Now fold from two sides and roll slightly, then from the opposite sides also. Lay a sheet of brown paper on a pan and put the paste on it. The pan should be large enough for the paste to lay in without doubling the paste. Set the pan on some broken ice, or on a large piece of ice, and cover it with another pan, and lay a few pieces of ice around on the top pan also. Let it remain this way half an hour, then roll it out, fold it and roll again, being careful not to roll too much; set on the ice again and let it remain twenty minutes, then roll again. Set on the ice again for fifteen minutes, roll again, and let remain on the ice for twenty minutes more, then roll out, handling the paste as little as possible with the hands. It should always be rolled in as cool a room as possible, and baked immediately after it is cut out. Bake in a moderately hot oven.

Tarts.

Roll out puff paste about ¼ inch thick, cut out with a large round cutter, and with a small cutter press gently in the middle of each one cut out. Cut out so as to have as little scrap as possible. When baked, press each tart down in the middle, and fill with cranberry sauce or apple marmalade.

Pie Crust.

Two lbs. flour, 1 lb. butter, a scant 1 pint water. The butter should be a stiff paste. Rub the butter and flour well together between the hands until fine, then pour the water over mixture. Ice water should be used in hot weather. Mix the water in as lightly as possible. Lard may be used in place of butter, but is not equal to it; when lard is used, add a pinch of salt. If the butter is too salty, wash out in cold water. Have the pie plates greased. With the scraper cut some of the dough into pieces large enough for bottom crusts, roll a little, just enough to make them round. Flatten a little with the palm of the hand. Before rolling out, dust the bench with flour. Roll out a little crosswise, lift up the dough, dust the bench, turn the dough upside down, and roll out lengthwise of the bench. Get it to a round flat shape with as little rolling as possible, as rolling it much will make it tough. Roll very little larger than the plate, so as not to have much scrap dough. Roll out about one-half of the dough for "bottoms." As soon as the bottom is rolled out for one pie put on the pie plate, lift up the pie plate about 3 inches and let fall again a couple of times, don't press it down with the fingers. Make the bottom crust for pies a little thicker than the top crust. Have plain pie plates, don't get those with a groove pressed in them. When making some juicy fruit pie wash the rims of the pies before putting on the top crust with water. If the oven should be a little cold, and you wish the pies to have a nice color, wash over with a brush dipped in the beaten yolks of eggs and a very little water.

Apple Pie.

Pare tart apples and cut fine. Fill up the pies, add white sugar to sweeten and a dust of ground cinnamon, or a little of the grated *yellow* of a lemon. Put a few tablespoonfuls water in each pie, also about ½ oz. fresh butter. Don't pare the apples until ready to make the pies, as they turn black looking. If you prefer the apples stewed, put into a stew pan with just enough water to cover them, stew until soft, then mash, sweeten and flavor to taste.

Cranberry Pie.

Wash the berries and pick out all that are not fit. Put into a stew pan with barely enough water to cover them, stew until soft, pour into a crock and let them cool. Then rub through a colander or sieve and sweeten, or sweeten while hot. The sugar should be sieved before putting it in; white sugar is best, although any kind of common sugar may be used. Fill the pie with the fruit, roll out the dough, cut it in strips and lay diagonally across, previously wetting the rim of the pie with a little water.

Mince Pie.

Mince meat procured from the groceries is generally too thick, and should be thinned with the addition of sweet cider. The best mince meat is made of beef, suet, apples, brown sugar, seedless raisins, currants, the grated *yellow* of lemons, a little citron, ground cinnamon, cloves and allspice, good sweet cider, and enough Port Wine to impart a good taste; the beef, apples, &c., to be chopped fine and then all thoroughly mixed.

Lemon Pies, No. 1.

Six good sized and fresh lemons, 3 lbs. white sugar, 6 eggs, 1 pint milk, ½ lb. corn starch, 2 oz. fresh butter, a pinch of salt, and 3 qts. water; put the sugar in a bowl, and grate on it the *yellow* of the lemons; don't use the white rind or seeds, or the pies will be bitter. Also squeeze the juice of the lemons on the sugar. Set the milk on the stove to boil, beat the eggs and corn starch together, and when the milk boils put this in, stirring briskly; then add the sugar and lemon juice. Be careful not to get it scorched. Put into a bowl to cool, and when cool fill the pies, cover and bake; or make the custard a little thicker, and fill the pies, not putting any crust on them. When baked, beat up some whites of eggs, add pulverized sugar, and spread this over the pies, and set in the oven to brown.

Lemon Pies, No. 2.

One good sized fresh lemon, 1 egg, ½ lb. white sugar, 2 heaping tablespoonfuls of flour, and 1 pint water; grate the *yellow* of the lemon into a bowl, put in the flour, then the egg, add a very little water, and beat this smooth with a spatula. Then add the sugar and water, stir well, fill the pies pretty full, wet the rim of the pie before putting on the top crust, and cut a good many holes in the top crust. This makes a good pie, but it sometimes boils out considerable while baking.

Cocoanut Custard Pie.

Grate the cocoanuts, add a little melted butter, enough sweet milk to make a right soft batter, and sweeten to taste. Bake without a top crust. Allow 2 eggs for each pie.

Pumpkin Custard Pie.

Pare and remove the seeds from the pumpkin, cut in small pieces, and stew until soft; put into a colander and allow all water to run off, then rub through the colander into a bowl. Add sugar to sweeten, some beaten eggs, about 1 for each pie, thin with boiled milk, flavor with ground allspice. Bake without a top crust.

FAMILY BAKING.

It seems to me there is not the interest taken by mothers to instruct their daughters in baking and cooking that there should be. It is often the case that a mother who has several grown-up daughters does the baking herself, and her daughters know very little about it. Ask her why she don't allow her daughters to do the baking, and she will probably tell you, "Oh, they have plenty of time yet to learn." It may be, and very often is, more convenient for families to buy their bread, but if every woman knew *how to bake good bread*, it would contribute much towards the health and happiness of all. None but those who have experienced it, know the mortification felt when the bread is bad after *trying their best*. There are a great number of women who can bake good bread, and I don't think they regret it, although it may not be considered *a high-toned accomplishment* by *some*. I think the formation of Ladies' Baking and Cooking Societies would be a good idea. It would be profitable to all. Have a meeting, say once a month, each member donating a specimen of her baking, bread or cake, and various "cooked dishes," the recipes for making them to be printed, and a copy distributed to each member. The business of the meeting, as remarks, essays, &c., on baking and cooking, could be concluded at an early hour in the evening, say by 9 o'clock, after which time a few hours could be agreeably spent in company with relatives and friends, previously inviting them to call, and having dancing, singing, or various social games, thus combining pleasure with profit.

The recipes herein mentioned are most of them adapted to families, as well as hotels and bakeries. The *ferment* mentioned as made with *stock yeast* is the *yeast* generally sold to families by bakers, and is used by the bakers themselves. Every large-sized family obliged to do their own baking should have a brick oven built, and covered with a shed to protect it from rain. A brick oven large enough to meet the requirements of a large family can be built at a comparatively small cost. It is often the case that a woman does the baking in a rickety old stove. The reason a great many women fail to make good bread is because they allow the sponge to fall too much or the dough to raise too much.

Ferment for Family Baking.

Put a few potatoes on to boil, about 6 good sized ones; put sufficient water on them, so that there will be plenty to *scald* a handful of flour; when they have boiled soft, put into a clean crock that has been well *scalded out* the handful of flour, and pour enough *scalding* water to make a smooth paste. Take the potatoes out and mash them, and add them also. If you want a good quantity of ferment, then add the hot water also, but if not, only add sufficient to make the ferment about milkwarm, or nearly cold in hot weather, and put in a gill of family yeast, or 4 cakes of "National Dry Yeast," made at Seneca, N. Y., or some other equally as good. When set with dry yeast, it will require longer for the ferment to rise and fall than with family yeast. Set the ferment on a shelf near the ceiling, where it will keep moderately warm, and where it will not be *disturbed*. Put it in a narrow crock. Make this in the evening, and set the sponge the next morning, or if it has not *fell yet*, wait until evening before setting sponge.

Setting Sponge and Making Dough.

Strain the ferment into a wooden bowl or small doughtray, add one-fourth as much milkwarm water as ferment, stir in sufficient sieved flour to make a rather stiff batter, let this set in a moderately warm place until the sponge has *raised and fell* a very little, then add three-fourths as much milkwarm water as you set ferment and *water* for sponge. Make into dough, and allow it to raise, which will take generally about one hour; then make into loaves and bake. Have the room while the sponge and dough are raising *comfortably* warm, but not warm enough to make you feel uncomfortable. Be careful that the sponge don't get disturbed while it is raising.

Family Yeast.

Take 6 good sized potatoes, pare them and boil until soft. then mash them in a narrow 2-gallon crock, and put on them about 1 lb. flour. Boil 1 handful of hops in a gallon of water for 15 minutes, and strain this while boiling on the flour and potatoes, stirring thoroughly until smooth. When about milkwarm, or nearly cold in summer, add 1 gill of good family yeast, stir well, and set in a moderately warm place. When it has raised and fell about 1 inch, stir it well; it is then ready for use. Set in a cool place; use 1 gill of this to ½ gallon milkwarm water, or cold water in summer, to set sponge. Set the crock in a tub of cold water to cool after the flour is scalded, in summer.

Pan Cakes.

Four heaping tablespoonfuls of flour, 4 eggs, a pinch of salt, sweet milk enough to make a soft batter; stir this well, and have it thin and smooth. Put a little lard in a skillet, and when it is hot put enough of the batter to make a thin cake. Bake a nice light brown color on both sides. Serve while hot.

Potato Cakes.

Take raw potatoes, pare and grate them, put in a very little flour, put in 3 eggs to each ½ gallon grated potatoes, and a little salt. Fry in hot lard until a nice brown on both sides. A little sweet cream may be added to the mixture, if desired. Serve while hot.

ICE CREAM.

For making ice cream, the cream should be sweet and good. Fresh cream makes a much better quality of ice cream than some that has been kept three or four days. After having eaten a dish of cream made from old cream, there will be a sort of buttery coating on the tongue and roof of the mouth. This will not occur if the ice cream is made of fresh cream, unless the ice cream is beaten too much. Ice cream should be made and kept, if possible, in a cool, shady place. The tin cans, when empty, should be well scalded and rinsed out; stand them up so the water will run out, then wipe thoroughly dry and lay on a shelf, keeping the lid off until well aired, then put the lid on. The cans should be nicely arranged on shelves. When the "season" is over, grease the cans inside and out before putting away. In about a week or two before the season begins, get everything in readiness; thoroughly clean the cans, have those that need mending taken away, be sure that none of them leak. See also that the tubs are in good condition and do not leak, and have good hoops, hinges and plugs. There are machines for breaking ice; if you have none, get a large stamper made of hard wood, or smaller if made of iron; have the ice cream tubs a little higher than the cans; get some cheap blue paint, and give the tubs a coating or two every spring. There should be a good deal of space between the can and tub for the ice. Don't mash the ice too fine; have a stout wooden box made of thick hard plank for breaking the ice in, and thoroughly put together, so that it will not come apart while breaking the ice.

To each gallon of cream take 1½ lbs. white sugar and 3 eggs. The eggs may be omitted, if desired. Beat up the eggs a little, pour on half the cream and put in the sugar; strain this through a strainer into the ice cream can. There will be a little sugar left in the strainer, pour the rest of the cream on this and stir; then put on the lid and pack ice around. Break up the ice, and sprinkle salt pretty thickly over it; any kind of coarse salt will do. Mix the salt and ice thoroughly before putting it around the can, with a strong scoop or shovel; after the ice is packed around the can, turn the can about 10 minutes, then scrape down the cream from the sides of the can with a pallet knife, and turn again, and so on, scraping down every 10 minutes until the cream gets pretty stiff; then let a little of the water out of the tub (have a plug at the bottom of the tub with which to let off the water), and pack more salted ice around the can, beat up with a paddle for about 20 minutes, put in the flavor, beat about 10 minutes longer, scrape off the paddle *lightly*, and scrape the ice cream down from the sides of the can, so as to have it level. If not wanted right away, let all the water out of the tub, cover the can with salted ice. Ice cream is best when it stands packed about an hour after being made.

One gallon of good cream will make 1½ gallons ice cream. If it is beaten more than this, it becomes buttery. For flavoring with vanilla, use 2 good-sized vanilla beans to 5 gallons ice cream, cut in small pieces and put into a tin can, pour on about ¾ pint of water, let it boil until very little water remains in the can, but be careful not to burn it; have a lid on the can while boiling it. Strain this when cool through a fine muslin rag into the ice cream. Put that which remains in the rag into a bottle, and pour enough alcohol on to cover it, then cork. This will make a good extract. Vanilla flavoring is generally preferred. Remember always to put *salt* on ice for making ice cream, and be sure that the *tub does not leak*. Some ice cream makers allow the cream to come to a boil before beginning to freeze it. Others use *milk* and scalded corn starch. Ice cream cans that have round iron bottoms ("Manigle's patent," I believe) are the best when turning by hand.

This recipe is for making ice cream with the common can, hand or steam freezer. Remember that the ice cream should not be beaten until *rather stiff*. There are also porcelain cans and porcelain-lined cans for keeping ice cream. Always attend to ice cream, so that it does not get soft, putting salted ice around it, and beating smooth with the paddle. Should it get soft and full of lumps, strain it and freeze as before.

Strawberry Ice Cream.

Take 1 qt. strawberries, mash them and put them in 1 gallon of ice cream, and beat up thoroughly; a little red coloring may be added, if it is desired to have it of a fine red color. Made in this way, no one will complain that the ice cream is not made with the fruit. Or, to 3 qts. good fresh cream add 2 lbs. sugar, stir it well, and then put in 1 qt. strawberry juice that has been obtained from "dead ripe" strawberries. Freeze in the usual way.

Chocolate Ice Cream.

Scrape down some cocoa, put into a clean pan with a little water, set on the stove or in the oven, and work with a spoon until smooth; then strain through a sieve into the ice cream. Flavor to suit the taste.

Lemon Ice Cream.

Flavor with oil of lemon.

Pine Apple Ice Cream.

Cut up a pine apple into fine pieces, sprinkle sugar thickly over it, and mash it well with a wooden stamper; then strain into 1 gallon ice cream that has been made by using 2 lbs. of sugar to 1 gallon of cream.

Orange Water Ice.

One doz. oranges, 1 gallon water; grate the *yellow* rind from 6 of the oranges, add a little of the grated rind, and strain it through a fine muslin cloth into the balance of the water; add 2 lbs. sugar, and freeze the same as ice cream. It does not require to be beaten like ice cream; just stir with the paddle until smooth.

Pine Apple Water Ice

Is made in the same manner as the ice cream, using water instead of cream, and adding ½ lb. more sugar.

Gum Paste for a Pyramid.

Take 4 oz. picked gum tragacanth, pour on about 1¼ pints water. Do this in the evening, and let it stand until the next morning; then strain through a clean coarse cloth into a large bowl, add lozenge sugar until pretty thick, stir well with the spatula; then put in more sugar until rather stiff. Throw out on a clean marble slab or table, and work with the hands. Tie up a little corn starch in a clean white rag, and dust the slab or bench with this. This paste may be colored to suit the fancy. Roll out with the rolling pin, and cut after any desired pattern. Put in a warm place to dry. Then set together and ornament with icing; a very nice ornament can thus be made for the supper table or show window. This quantity is sufficient to make a very large pyramid, and will keep a long time if put in a crock and covered tightly. Keep in a cool place. When it is desired to keep it, put sufficient sugar into the strained gum to make it pretty thick, but not stiff;

then when wanted for use, a little may be taken out, and more sugar worked in until stiff enough.

Red "Sugar Sand."

Take clean granulated sugar, and put into a bowl, add some carmine that has been dissolved in a little alcohol, or use a little prepared cochineal. Rub the sugar between the hands, and a fine red or pink color may be obtained in this way. Set in a warm place, and while drying rub between the hands occasionally, so it will not form into lumps.

Any color of "sugar sand" may be made in this manner by using colors that are not poisonous, always being careful to dry on a shady place with a very moderate heat.

To Open Cocoanuts.

Have a hard wooden block; it should have a hollow, so the cocoanut will lay in a little. Take a sharp hatchet, and with the corner chip off a piece of the shell at the ends where the holes are, when the balance of the shell may be easily taken off by chipping off in small pieces. Turn the nut occasionally while chipping off. Then wash the hands clean and pare off the fine skin with a sharp knife or "spoke shave."

To Prevent Windows Being Frosted.

Wash with brandy or alcohol.

Taffy.

Take 1 gal. N. O. molasses, 2½ lbs. white sugar, ½ lb. fresh butter; boil, and when it gets thick, stir to prevent burning. Boil to a crack, which may be known by taking out a little on the end of the stick, previously dipping the end of the stick in water, then dip in right cold water again. If it cracks while attempting to squeeze it in the hand, it has boiled sufficient. Pour this upon a marble slab that has been previously cleaned and *slightly* greased. There should be square iron or steel rods laid around the edges, to prevent the mass running off the slab. Do not handle it until the edges of the mass commence to harden; then with both hands lay each side of the taffy to the middle of the mass. Let it remain in this manner until it is cool enough to be handled; then pull it until light. Have a little flour at hand, and flour the hands to prevent the mass from sticking. Pull the taffy on a large iron hook fastened well to a post, and known as a "candy hook;" grease the hook *very lightly*. If the mass is handled or stirred much before it is ready to pull, it is liable to "grain." When ready to pull, do so briskly for a short time. If it should appear to "fall to pieces" when put on the hook, the slab has been greased too heavy. In this case keep pulling the mass for a short time, no difference if it does appear to be rotten, and it will be all right. If the taffy is intended to be made into sticks, boil until the mass will not stick to the teeth while chewing. If it is desired to have it striped, let a little of the mass lie on the slab until the others are pulled, roll that which has been pulled to a short stick, and lay the other on this in long strips, an even distance apart. Now take hold of one end of the roll with the right hand, and pull it out lengthwise until the desired thickness is obtained, then pinch or cut it off, twist the stick a little and roll until round, and so continue on with the rest, rolling those that have been pulled first, to keep them in a round shape; sprinkle a little pulverized sugar on the bench before rolling out; for a small quantity a pan may be used instead of a marble slab, when the slab is not to be had. This taffy will not keep well in summer.

Apple Jelly.

Take tart apples, wash them clean, and cut each apple in three or four pieces; put them into a kettle with only sufficient water to cover them. When they have boiled right soft, throw them into a close willow basket, and allow the juice to drain through into a clean tub or other vessel. Boil the apples in the evening, and let them drain through until next morning. To each quart of juice take 1½ lbs. best white sugar, put into a clean copper or porcelain-lined kettle, and boil until it jellies, which may be known by putting a little in a saucer and setting on ice or cold water. While boiling, skim the jelly with a skimmer. It may also be colored a brilliant red or yellow.

A great amount of the jelly now sold in tumblers for currant, raspberry, quince, orange, &c., is nothing but apple jelly colored and flavored with the various extracts.

Currant Jelly.

Take currants that are right ripe; to each pint of juice use 1 lb. best white sugar, boil briskly, and skim while boiling. It should not boil longer than about twenty minutes, or it will become *stringy.* Wash the kettle out clean before boiling again. When making jellies be careful not to allow them to boil over. If not red enough, aniline coloring may be used, but care should be taken not to use too much, as it is poisonous.

Virgin Yeast, No. 1.

Fill a clean candy jar half full of stock yeast, put it on a shelf near the ceiling where it is moderately warm, and where it will not be disturbed, cover air tight and allow it to stand three days, when it is ready for use. (Put into the jar just after the malt is put in and before the stock yeast is in.)

Virgin Yeast, No. 2.

Two oz. hops, 1½ lbs. flour, 1½ gall. water; let the hops boil in the water fifteen minutes; scald the flour with some of the hop water and make a soft, smooth paste, stirring it well, then strain on the balance of the hop water; when milkwarm put in a heaping tablespoonful of salt and 1 of brown sugar; stir well; put in a crock, set in a moderately warm place and allow it to set three days. Boil 2 lbs. pared potatoes, mash and add them, and let stand another day.

Aniline Coloring.

Put aniline in alcohol, shake well, and allow it to stand a few days. Care should be taken in using this, as it is poisonous.

Yellow Coloring.

Mix gamboge with a little water in a saucer. This is also said to be poisonous, but when used in small quantities will do no harm.

Prepared colors made especially for bakers and confectioners, are generally to be had in a confectioners' furnishing store.

Macaroons.

Two lbs. almonds that have been blanched and dried, 4 lbs. dry white sugar, about 23 whites of eggs. Rub the almonds and whites of eggs in a stone mortar, then work in the sugar well, run out on brown paper laid on a pan and bake in a very cool oven.

Small Charlotte Russe.

Beat up a pound mixture as mentioned for sponge cakes. Spread about ¼ or ½ thick on a sheet of brown paper laid on a pan, bake it light; when cool cut out, and line small tin cups with this, and join with icing. Allow it to dry in the cups, then take out and fill with whipped cream. Have the best of cream; put it into a tin bucket, and set the bucket on some broken ice, putting a little salt on the ice first, and stirring it well. Beat up the cream with the egg beater, and add sufficient pulverized sugar to sweeten. Flavor with extract of vanilla. This should be made shortly before it is wanted.

It is my purpose at some future time to enlarge this work. I would therefore be thankful to any person disposed to give me useful information in regard to baking, &c.

Respectfully,

THE AUTHOR.

INDEX.

PAGE.

Almond Puffs....................43
Aniline Coloring....................61
Apple Cake....................17
Apple Pie....................48
Apple Jelly....................61
Articles and Utensils—where to procure....................19

Bakeshop, the.................... 7
Baking with Fleischmann's Compressed Yeast....................18
Bread.................... 8
Brown Scotch, No. 1....................31
Brown Scotch, No. 2....................31
Brown Jumbles....................32
Buns....................15

Candy Ornaments, for Macaroon Pyramid....................42
Chocolate Sponge Drop....................34
Chocolate Ice Cream....................57
Cinnamon Cake....................16
Citron Cake....................39
Cocoanut Custard Pie....................50
Cranberry Pie....................48
Cream Puffs....................29
Crullers....................38
Cup Cake....................31
Currant Cake....................39
Currant Jelly....................61
Custard for Cream Puffs....................30

Doughnuts....................17
Drop Cake....................26

PAGE.

Family Baking......51
Family Yeast......53
Ferment......11
Ferment, without Stock Yeast......18
Ferment for Family Baking......52
French Bread......14
Fruit Cake......23

Ginger Cakes......39
Ginger Snaps......37
Ginger S's......38
Graham Bread......14
Gum Paste for a Pyramid......58

Hints on Making Cakes......19

Ice Cream......54
Icing......43

Jelly Cake......26
Jelly Roll......36
Jenny Lind Cakes......35

Lady Cake......22
Lady Fingers......27
Large Sponge Cake......26
Lemon Ice Cream......57
Lemon Pie, No. 1......49
Lemon Pie, No. 2......50
Lemon Cake......28

Macaroons......63
Macaroon Pyramid......40
Making Dough......12
Making Dough, Family Baking......53
Mince Pie......49
Molasses Cup Cake......33

PAGE.
Molasses Pound Cake..36
Mountain Cake..23

Orange Water Ice..58

Pan Cakes..54
Paris Cakes..25
Pie Crust..47
Pine Apple Ice Cream..57
Pine Apple Water Ice..58
Potato Cake..54
Pound Cake..21
Puff Paste..40
Pumpkin Custard Pie..50

Red "Sugar Sand"..59
Remarks..5
Rolls..16
Rough and Readys..37
Rusks or Light Cakes..15
Rye Bread..13

Scrap Cake..39
Setting Sponge..53
Small Charlotte Russe..63
Small Sponge Cake..30
Soda Biscuit, No. 1..46
Strawberry Ice Cream..57
Stock Yeast..9
Sponge Biscuit..29
Sugar Cake..39
Substitute for Whites of Eggs in making Icing..45

Taffy..59
Tarts..47
Taylor Cakes, No. 1..34

PAGE.

Taylor Cakes, No. 2 34
To Open Cocoanuts 59
To Prevent Windows being Frosted 59
To Set Sponge 11
To Make an Egg Beater 42
Twist 15

Virgin Yeast, No. 1 61
Virgin Yeast, No. 2 61

Wash to impart a Gloss to Buns, Rolls, &c 17
Water Icing 45
White Jumbles 31
White Scotch Cakes 33
Wine Cake 33

Yellow Coloring 61

www.ingramcontent.com/pod-product-compliance
Lightning Source LLC
Chambersburg PA
CBHW021516090426
42739CB00007B/633